Ulysses S. (Ulysses Simpson) Grant, Fitz-John Porter

Appeal to the President of the United States for a Re-Examination of the Proceedings of the General Court Martial

Ulysses S. (Ulysses Simpson) Grant, Fitz-John Porter

Appeal to the President of the United States for a Re-Examination of the Proceedings of the General Court Martial

ISBN/EAN: 9783744660167

Printed in Europe, USA, Canada, Australia, Japan

Cover: Foto ©ninafisch / pixelio.de

More available books at **www.hansebooks.com**

CONTENTS.

PRINTED DOCUMENTS ACCOMPANYING APPEAL:

MORRISTOWN, N. J., *June 21st*, 1869.

General WILLIAM T. SHERMAN,
Commanding Army of the United States.

GENERAL:—The President of the United States having assured my friends, who have recently brought my case to his notice, that "if injustice had been done me it should be righted," and intimated a purpose of primarily obtaining the opinion of the Hon. Secretary of War and yourself, as to the mode of redress under given circumstances, I have deemed it proper to have put in print the papers relating to my case, with a view of facilitating your examination of them.

The President, Secretaty of War and yourself, having achieved the highest honors which successful generalship ever receives from our people, I could not covet an investigation, and, if practicable a decision in my case, from any superior tribunal.

My desire to have the whole case as it now stands, adjudicated by soldiers, will be fully met by a decision rendered by the President, the Secretary of War and yourself, if such a mode be, as I trust it may be, found practicable.

I am, General,

With high respect,

Your obedient servant,

FITZ JOHN PORTER.

TO THE

PRESIDENT OF THE UNITED STATES

FOR A

Re-Examination of the Proceedings

OF THE

GENERAL COURT MARTIAL

IN HIS CASE,

BY

MAJ. GEN'L FITZ JOHN PORTER,

WITH ACCOMPANYING DOCUMENTS.

MORRISTOWN, N. J.
1869.

APPEAL TO THE PRESIDENT.

MORRISTOWN, N. J., *June* 10*th*, 1869.

GENL. WILLIAM T. SHERMAN, *Head Quarters of the Army, Washington, D. C.*

SIR:—I apply to you as General Commanding the Army, to transmit to the President, and to recommend to his favorable consideration, this, my application to him :

1st. To remit the sentence of the Court Martial now in force against me of disqualification "forever to hold any office of trust or profit under the Government of the United States :"

2nd. To be nominated to the Senate for restoration to my rank in the Army, under the late act of Congress allowing that mode of redress of wrong by a Court Martial.

I beg to ask, most respectfully, your intervention in my application to the President, because, in the first place, I desire to put my case before him upon its merits unwarped and unencumbered by political or party passion, and, in the next place, because I seek to be judged as a soldier, by soldiers whose judgment the country will respect, and history accept as true and final.

With due elimination from the investigation of all matters not pertinent to the charges, I am prepared to satisfy such a tribunal that my sentence was unjust. I have newly discovered evidence which conclusively establishes how false was the principal accusation.

It is matter of general information that the allegations against me were inspired by the failure of General Pope's campaign in Virginia. His friends undertook to maintain that he committed no error ; and to attribute the result of his operations to the defection and treasonable misconduct of certain officers and soldiers of the Army of the Potomac who preferred to be commanded by General McClellan. The formal charges were

1862, of the condition of the enemy in my front was correct, I am satisfied that the documents herewith submitted will convince the President, that the sentence against me was on all points against the clear weight of evidence in the case.

As a portion of the documents on which I make this application, through you, to the President, I submit beside the record of the court, a review thereof by Judge-Advocate-General Holt; a commentary on the latter by my counsel on the trial, Mr. Reverdy Johnson; letters from Generals Longstreet and Wilcox and Colonel Charles Marshall, A. D. C., and certain Confederate reports; a review of this last named evidence by Doctor Guernsey; and finally General Pope's protest against a rehearing of my case, with my reply thereto.

I would prefer in offering Mr. Johnson's Review, to modify some passages in which he has expressed warmly his generous estimation of my services, and his strong condemnation of the extreme and unparalled injustice with which I have been treated. But, as I deem it proper also to lay before you, an anonymous pamphlet in reply thereto, written I am informed by Judge-Advocate Holt, I ought not to withhold anything in the kind judgment of Mr. Johnson concerning me and my case, which may be Mr. Holt's provocation and defence for the mode in which I am denounced by him, in his elaborate style of invective. The language used by Mr. Holt will, I am sure, suggest to you, and to the President, that one whose official partiality manifests itself by such proofs, ought not now to deal officially with my case.

For the vindication of my conduct as a true and faithful officer, and of my name and honor, before the country I have endeavored to serve, I am chiefly concerned to have your judgment and the judgment of the President. And in this relation I am glad to be permitted to submit herewith a brief but comprehensive opinion on my case by General McClellan and by him handed to me for your perusal.

I am General,

Very respectfully

Your ob't sv't.,

FITZ JOHN PORTER.

GEN. McCLELLAN'S OPINION.

In the case of General Fitz John Porter, two points seem to have been chiefly relied upon to justify the verdict :

1st. The alleged failure to obey the order of 6.30 P. M., August 27th, requiring him to move his command at 1 A. M. of the 28th.

2nd. The alleged failure to attack on the 29th August.

It appears to me that the first point, considered by itself, can be disposed of very briefly. Porter's troops were much fatigued and needed rest; the night was very dark ; the road bad and blocked by wagon trains.

Porter's impulse was to obey the order literally, but his subordinate Generals (Morell, Sykes, and Butterfield), were so decided in their conviction that the march should be delayed, that he yielded to their advice, and started only at three o'clock. The result showed that a still greater delay would have been judicious, as giving the troops more rest, and bringing them to their destination quite as early as they actually reached it—for they were much delayed on the march. It is not charged that any injury to the service resulted from the postponement, and it may confidently be asserted that no unprejudiced officer of experience would maintain that Gen. Porter's action in the case warrants the severe sentence passed upon him. He simply exercised a responsibility that must sometimes be taken by an officer receiving an order from a superior at a distance. With sufficient reasons, and from good motives, he departed slightly from the literal requirements of the order, while he thoroughly carried out its spirit ; his purpose was to reach the end of the march in the shortest time, with the least fatigue to his men, and to keep them in proper condition for action. This may have been an error of judgment (I do not think it was), but surely cannot be regarded as a crime.

Now, as to the second point, viz. : the alleged failure to attack the enemy on the 29th of August.

Up to about the hour of noon on that day, Gen. McDowell was with or near Gen. Porter, and, as the senior officer, was vested with the command. He had under his control two divisions of his own corps—those of King and Ricketts. About noon he separated himself from Porter, and, with his two divisions, marched off to join Pope, by a road leading to the left and rear of Porter's position.

It is clear that up to the hour of noon the responsibility for any failure to attack rested with McDowell, not with Porter.

I do not think it necessary to consider here the question whether Gen. McDowell ought to or could have attacked with the joint commands. I merely say that up to the period of his departure Porter cannot be held responsible. Porter's responsibility commences, therefore, about noon. The strength of his command, after the departure of King's and Rickett's divisions, was about 12,000—somewhat less. Porter believed at the time, from his own observation, the statements of prisoners, and other sources, that Longstreet was in front of him with greatly superior force.

The positive evidence is now attainable to prove that Longstreet *was* in position with his whole command (more than double Porter's corps in strength) before noon on the 29th, ready and anxious to be attacked, and, therefore, that Porter's opinions were correct. It appears clear that the only opportunity of attacking, with good chances of success and decisive results, was early in the forenoon, and with all the combined forces of Gens. McDowell and Porter.

As soon as the whole of Longstreet's command was in position, the result of such an attack became doubtful.

For Porter to have made it, after the withdrawal of McDowell's two divisions, would have been absolute madness ; for to have attacked, with less than 12,000 men, a force more than double in number, excellent in quality, and strongly posted, would have ensured the complete repulse of the attacking party, with heavy loss.

That attacks must sometimes be made under such circumstances is no doubt true, for it is sometimes necessary for a portion of an army to sacrifice itself to save the rest of the army, or an important part of it. But it does not appear that this was such a case. The right of our army was abundantly able to take care of itself, and was not hard pressed at the time in question. The mere position of Porter's command accomplished the very important result of keeping at least double his numbers in front of him, and paralyzed them so far as any action against our right was concerned. The additional evidence now attainable (which could not be had at the time of the trial) proves beyond question that Gen. Pope was mistaken in the belief, which he then entertained, that Longstreet was still remote from the field of battle, and that Porter had only a small force in his front; it proves that an attack made by Porter at any time after Gen. McDowell's departure would, in all probability —it might be said *with certainty*, were there any such thing as absolute certainty in war—have resulted in a complete repulse, with great and useless sacrifice of life; it proves that Porter's arrangements were excellent, since they enabled him to hold a greatly superior force in check; it proves that, far from meriting the severe sentence imposed upon him, he in fact deserved great praise for his conduct on that day.

Justice requires that Gen. Porter's conduct on the 30th, when, as is acknowledged, he fought his corps most energetically and desperately, should be kept in mind when forming an opinion of the transactions of the 29th, especially in the light of the new evidence now adduced.

GEO. B. McCLELLAN.

June 4, 1869.

2

———◆———

To the Editor of the World:

In the course of my studies on the history of the war, I have had occasion to investigate minutely the facts in the case of General Fitz John Porter. The conclusions to which I have come, and the data upon which they are based, are set forth in the following paper.

ALFRED H. GUERNSEY.

New York, *July 2nd*, 1866.

On the 27th of November, 1862, a court-martial was convened for the trial of Major-General Fitz John Porter, charged with grave military offences. After an investigation which lasted forty-five days, the accused was found guilty upon both charges and nearly all the specifications brought against him, and was sentenced *" to be cashiered, and to be forever disqualified from holding any office of trust or honor under the government of the United States."*

I believe, and shall endeavor to show, that this finding of the court was unwarranted by the evidence as presented on the trial, and by the facts in the case which can now be proven. In discussing this proposition, although much unpublished evidence has fallen into my hands, I shall not resort to other than official documents of admitted validity. The authorities which I shall cite are—the " Proceedings of the Fitz John Porter Court-Martial," which will be cited as " *Court-Martial ;*" General Pope's Report of his Campaign, cited as "*Pope's Rep.*," which embodies many sub-reports; and General R. E. Lee's Report of the " Operations of the Army of Northern Virginia," cited as *Reb. Rec.*, embodying many sub-reports. The two former documents are published by authority of the Congress of the United States; the last by authority of the Confederate Congress, and republished in Putnam's Rebellion Record, vol. 9.

The alleged acts of disobedience were committed on the 28th and 29th of August, 1862. Up to that time, it is conceded by the prosecution that the military record of Fitz John Porter was highly honorable. Commissioned as Colonel in May, 1861, he had risen in ten months to the command of an army corps, as Major-General. His services during the Peninsular campaign were certainly inferior to those of no other commander in the Army of the Potomac. Two of the five great battles which marked the "seven days" were fought by him; and for his services at Malvern Hill, General McClellan wrote to the Secretary of War that, if there were another grade to add to that of Major-General, he would ask it for Porter. I shall have occasion to show that from the 30th of August onward his military conduct did not belie his former reputation.

On the 27th of August Jackson had turned the right of Pope, fallen upon his rear, captured his principal depot of supplies at Manassas, and endangered his communications with the capital. Porter, with his corps, had just joined the army of Pope. He had that afternoon arrived at Warrenton Station, on the railroad, ten miles from Bristoe Station, where Hooker had just had a sharp encounter with Ewell's division of Jackson's corps. Pope, then at Bristoe, sent an order to Porter, of which the following is the essential part:

The Major-General commanding directs that you start at one o'clock to-night, and come forward with your whole corps, or such part of it as is with you, so as to be here by daylight to-morrow morning. Hooker has had a very severe action with the enemy, with a loss of about three hundred killed and wounded. The enemy has been driven back, but is retiring along the railroad. We must drive him from Manassas, and clear the country between that and Gainsville, where McDowell is. * * * * It is necessary, on all accounts, that you should be here by day-light. (*Court-Martial*, 6.)

This order, dated at 6.30 o'clock was received by Porter, at about 10 P. M. The distance to be reached was about ten miles. Between the two points was the railway, with a common country road, running sometimes on one side, sometimes on the other, and occasionally on both sides of the track. The region is somewhat broken, intersected by brooks and patches of wood, with here and there a swampy place. The road was also considerably encumbered by wagons. The night was overcast, with no moon visible. About midnight a rain set in, and it became extremely dark. Porter, after consultation with his generals, Morell, Sykes, and Butterfield, decided, for the above reasons, to postpone the commencement of the march until three o'clock, so that the troops would be fairly on their way at daylight. These essensial facts are proved by the testimony upon the trial. (See Court-Martial; testimony of Sykes, Morell, Griffin, Butterfield, and others, pp. 123, 144, 160, 162, 176, 185, etc.) These officers and others testified that Bristoe would have been reached sooner by starting at three o'clock than at one o'clock; that is, the fatigue, delay, and disorder arising during the two hours of absolute darkness would have more than counterbalanced the time which would, apparently, have been gained. As it was, the head of the column, owing to the obstructions, did not reach Bristoe till after nine o'clock. It required quite six hours, mostly of daylight, to perform a march which the letter of the order required to be accomplished in three hours of extreme darkness. It was, therefore, physically impossible to carry out the order to its full extent. The "disobedience" consisted of postponing for two hours the commencement of its execution. This deviation seems to me to have been one fairly within the discretion of a corps commander, who must have been aware of many circumstances which the commanding general, ten miles away, was unaware. The fact that this deviation was advised by officers of such acknowledged capacity and zeal, is presumptive evidence that it involved want neither of zeal nor capacity in Porter. In fact, as it happened, it made no difference whether Bristoe was reached at daylight or noon.

This charge would never have been brought except as a makeweight to the far more serious accusations arising from the transactions of the next day. To explain these I must describe the situation on the 29th of August, both as it appeared to Pope and Porter, and as it really was.

Jackson, whose force amounted to something more than 25,000, besides Stuart's cavalry, numbering 6,000, had taken up a strong position near the battle-field of Bull Run. Here he resolved to await the arrival of Longstreet, who, as he knew, was on the march to unite with him. Longstreet's command numbered twenty-one brigades (*Reb. Rec.* IX, 574). The average strength of a confederate brigade, at the beginning of these operations, a fortnight before, was about 2,500. Longstreet had as yet lost only a few scores in battle; but in his rapid march some had doubtless fallen out by the way, but his brigades must still have averaged 2,000, making his effective strength more than 40,000. Pope supposed him to be, on the morning of the 29th, at a distance of from thirty to forty-eight hours' march; for at that time he wrote to McDowell and Porter: "The indications are that the whole force of the enemy is moving in this direction at a pace that will bring them here by to-morrow night or the next morning." (*Pope's Rep.*, 241). This would give him a full day and a half to deal with Jackson alone.

At this time Pope had 50,000 men, so disposed that half of them could fall upon Jackson in front, while the other half should assail his right flank and rear; between these two forces he thought that Jackson must certainly be crushed before Longstreet could arrive. (Pope's Rep., 19, 20). Upon this supposition were based the orders of the morning and afternoon of the 29th, the failure to carry out which forms the ground of the second charge against Porter. But, as I shall show beyond question, Longstreet at that moment, so far from being a day and a half or two days' distant from Jackson, was on the point of uniting, and had actually in effect united with him.

It is no part of my present purpose to criticise Pope's campaign, except in so far as relates to the special matter in hand, which is the conduct of Porter. But in order to elucidate this, I must endeavor to give a general idea of the topography of the region in which the operations of August 29 and 30 were carried on, and of the position of the forces engaged in those operations.

The Bull Run Mountains run nearly north and south, and are cloven by two gaps, Thoroughfare and Hopewell, about three miles apart. Jackson had marched up the western side of this range, crossed it at Thoroughfare Gap, and swooped down upon Pope's rear. Longstreet was following upon the same track. From the mountains, the country slopes eastward toward Bull Run River, the distance between the mountains and the river at the Stone Bridge being ten or twelve miles. The intervening plain, known as that of Manassas, is wooded and often rugged,

The Warrenton turnpike crosses this plain from northeast to southwest; the Manassas Gap Railroad crosses it from southeast to northwest; the railroad and turnpike intersect each other at Gainesville, a village about midway between the mountains and river. Let this figure ( ) serve to represent these features, now become historical. The line running downwards from right to left stands for the turnpike; that running upwards from right to left, the railroad. The lower right hand corner is Manassas Junction; the upper right hand corner is the Stone Bridge, five miles distant. At the intersection of the two lines is Gainesville; at the upper left hand corner, Thoroughfare Gap. Just below the turnpike, a mile from the Stone Bridge, is the first Bull Run battle-field; just above it, two miles farther west, is that of the second Bull Run, more properly called Groveton, from a hamlet there situated. In fact, both battle-fields cross the turnpike, but the first was mainly below, the second mainly above. The distances, as closely as we can measure them upon the large government map used upon the trial, are: Thoroughfare Gap to Gainesville, five miles; Gainesville to Groveton, four miles; Groveton to Stone Bridge, three miles; Manassas to Gainesville seven miles.

Now, on the morning of August 29, Jackson, with 25,000 men, was drawn up, his right at Groveton, his line extending northward about two miles. Directly in his front was half of Pope's force under Reynolds, Sigel, Heintzleman, and Reno, twenty-five thousand strong. The other half, of equal strength, under McDowell and Porter, lay along the Manassas Railroad from the Junction part way to Gainesville. According to Pope's belief, Longstreet was still west of the Bull Run Mountains, although, as I shall have to show, he was by nine o'clock in the morning east of the mountains as far as Gainesville, and so within four miles of the battle-field at Groveton, where an artillery contest at long range had been going on for several hours.

Early on the morning of the 29th, Pope, being then at Centreville, farther from Porter than was Longstreet, sent an order to Porter and McDowell, of which the following are the essential portions, the omitted parts being explanantory of matters which do not concern the present inquiry:

You will please move forward with your joint commands toward Gainsville. Heintzelman, Sigel, and Reno are moving on the Warrenton turnpike, *and must now be not far from Gainesville*. I desire that as soon as communication is established between this force and your own, the whole command shall halt. It may be necessary to fall back behind Bull Run to Centreville to-night. I presume it will be so on account of our supplies. * * * *If any considerable advantages are to be gained by departing from this order, it will not be strictly carried out.* One thing must be held in view, that the troops must occupy a position from which they can reach Bull Run to-night or by morning. The indications are that the whole force of the enemy is moving in this direction at a pace which will bring them here *by to-morrow night or the next day.* [*Court-Martial,* 7.]

General McDowell happened at that time to be in the position of a corps commander without any troops under him. Of his two divisions, one, that of Ricketts, had been detached from the main column and sent to Thoroughfare Gap to bar the passage of Longstreet. It was too late, and had been driven back on the previous evening by Longstreet, who was already through the Gap. McDowell's other division, that of King, but now commanded by Hatch, had been temporarily attached to Porter's corps. McDowell, who had been at Manasses Junction all the morning, came up with Porter about noon, and, in virtue of his rank as senior general, took command of the whole force. Here some conversation ensued between the two generals. McDowell, as is testified to by Colonel Locke and Captain Martin (*Court-Martial,* 135 *and* 141), said to Porter, " You are too far out ; this is no place to fight a battle." McDowell, however, testified that he had no recollection of having said this. The two generals then rode apart, when McDowell gave an order to Porter, respecting which there is an irreconcilable difference of statement. McDowell testifies (*Ibid,* 85) that Porter, pointing in the direction where the joint order directed them to move, said, " We cannot go in there anywhere without getting into a fight." McDowell at the time understood the remark to mean simply that Porter supposed the enemy was in his immediate front, not that he was indisposed to fight. (*Ibid,* 89.) He then directed Porter to " put his force in there," while he himself took King's division of his own corps in another direction. Porter asserts that the order was that he should remain where he was. (*Ibid,* 290.)

While it must be admitted that McDowell's positive testimony proves that he gave, or intended to give, the order as stated by him, everything that followed shows that Porter must have understood it as stated by himself. But it is not necessary to dwell upon this point, for the charge against Porter is, not that he disobeyed the order of McDowell, whatever it was, but that he disobeyed the joint order of Pope. McDowell, with his men, left that part of the field, and then, as he himself says (*Ibid*, 92), Porter ceased to be under his orders, and came directly under those of Pope, their common superior, and especially under the joint order, which, being the last received, superseded others previously given. This order enjoined two things—McDowell and Porter were to move their joint commands towards Gainsville, so as to form a connection with the forces of Sigel and Heintzelman and others, who were supposed to be near that place; and they must occupy a position from which they could reach Bull Run that night. Now, Sigel, Heintzelman, and the others, instead of being near Gainesville, were held in check by Jackson fully four miles to the east, and every rod marched in the prescribed direction would have removed McDowell and Porter further from a junction, besides rendering more difficult the other condition of being able to reach Bull Run that night. The order expressly provided that either or both generals to whom it was jointly addressed should deviate from it if important advantages would thereby be gained. Both did so. McDowell, instead of moving west toward Gainesville, moved north toward Groveton. The propriety of his so doing does not appear to have been brought in question. Porter, likewise using the discretion permitted by the order, deviated from its terms by remaining where he was. I shall endeavor to show that he also was fully justified in so doing; and that the same holds good in regard to a later order from Pope, the failure to comply with which forms the real burden of the charges against Porter.

The order was as follows:

Your line of march brings you in on the enemy's right flank. I desire you to push forward into action at once on the enemy's flank, and, if possible, on his rear, keeping your right in communication with General Reynolds. The enemy is massed in the woods in front of us, but can be shelled out as soon as you

enagage their flank. Keep heavy reserves, and use your batteries, keeping well closed to your right and rear all the time.
In case you are obliged to fall back, do so to your right and
rear, so as to keep you in close communication with the right
wing. (*Court Martial*, 7.)

The joint order left much to the discretion of those to whom
it was addressed. The last was peremptory, and failure to comply with it can be justified only on the ground of urgent military necessity or impossibility of execution. This order was
written at half-past four. The aid-de-camp who bore it thinks
it was delivered about five, but three unimpeached witnesses
(*Court Martial*, 127, 130, 136) show that the time was about
half-past six.

Both orders are based upon the supposition that the "whole
force" of the enemy under Longstreet was full twenty-four
hours distant ; that Jackson's corps was the only body to be encountered ; and that the Union force consequently was nearly
double that of the confederates. Whereas, I shall undertake
to show that Longstreet had united with Jackson fully four
hours before the last order was written, and six hours before it
was received, giving the confederates a preponderance of three
to two ; that the line of march prescribed to Porter would have
brought him almost directly upon the real confederate centre,
instead of upon its right flank and rear, as Pope presumed ;
and that the execution of the order would have involved the
annihilation of Porter's corps, and could hardly have failed to
result in the destruction of the entire Union army. I shall show
that Porter knew the essential facts in the case, that Pope did
not, and that consequently he was fully justified in not comply-
ing with the order.

The confederate reports embodied in Lee's Report enable us
to ascertain the positions and movements of his force during
the 29th of August.

On the evening of the 28th, Longstreet's whole force bivou-
acked on the east side of the Bull Run Mountains, the main
body passing through Thoroughfare Gap, the others through
Hopewell Gap, three miles to the north, having encountered,
from Ricketts, a slight opposition at the former place, which
cost them only twenty-five men, killed and wounded (*Reb. Rec.*
IX, 636). "Early on the morning of the 29th the columns were

3

united, and the march to join Jackson was resumed," says Longstreet (*Ibid*, 570). Hood (*Ibid*, 633) fixes the hour when the march was begun. He says, "'The next morning at daylight the march was resumed, this division in the advance." Daylight at this season is about 4.30. The head of the column could easily have reached Gainesville, five or six miles distant, by eight o'clock. That it did so is shown by General Buford, in command of the Union cavalry, who at nine o'clock saw a large force marching out of Gainesville, directly in the direction where the cannonading was then going on near Groveton, three or four miles distant. He counted seventeen regiments of infantry, one battery, and about five hundred cavalry. He estimated the regiments at about eight hundred each, which would give quite fourteen thousand men then close upon the field. (*Court-Martial*, 84, 188.) He reported this at once to McDowell, who received the report and communicated it to Porter about noon. (*Ibid*, 84.) Pope, however, does not appear to have received this report until evening, long after he had given his order to Porter to attack. (*Ibid, p.* 35.)

But these troops which Buford saw marching to the field were only a part of the confederate force pressing in the same direction. Wilcox, who commanded that portion which had passed through Hopewell Gap, says (*Reb. Rec.* IX. 641) that his force, at 9.30, united with the others at a point about two miles west of Gainesville. So that, before ten o'clock, the rear of Longstreet's corps was within five miles of the field, and the head— Hood's division—must have actually made a junction with Jackson. Quite half a score of the confederate commanders speak of the rapidity with which this ten miles' march, beginning at daylight, was performed. "Early in the day" is the phrase used by several in speaking of the time when they came upon the field (*e. g.* Hood, in *Ibid*, 633); and D. R. Jones, whose march was farthest to his position on the extreme right, says (*Ibid*, 636) that he arrived on the ground "about noon." Citations to this effect might be greatly multiplied, all showing that the junction of Longstreet with Jackson was fairly made by ten o'clock, and that by noon the line which was now the confederate right and centre was fully established. John Esten Cooke, in the "Life of Stonewall Jackson," gives the precise statement of the facts in the case. He says: "All the morning General

Longstreet was coming into position." Lee and Longstreet note specifically the positions and movements of eleven brigades of infantry, besides artillery, all belonging to Longstreet's corps, who were posted in this line, and moved in various ways to meet what they supposed to be the exigencies of the moment, and all considerably before the hour when Pope ordered the grand assault of the afternoon upon Jackson's left. Pope (*Report.* 21), says he gave the order at 5.30 ; but Grover, who bore the most brilliant part in the attack, says (*Ibid*, 77) that he received the order at three. The confederate reports place this attack still earlier. Thus Jackson (*Reb. Rec.*, IX. 578) says : " About two o'clock, P. M., the federal infantry in large force advanced to the attack on our left, occupied by the division under General Hill ; " and Ferno (*Ibid*, 652) says that his brigade " occupied the right of our line until *after the arrival of Longstreet*, when we rejoined our division in the centre ; and at 3.30 were ordered to advance, and soon after engaged the enemy." Jackson says (*Ibid*, 578) : " During the day, the commanding general arrived, and also General Longstreet with his command." Lee says (*Ibid*, 277) : " *After the arrival of Longstreet*, the enemy changed his position, and *began* to concentrate opposite Jackson's left, opening a brisk artillery fire."

These citations show that Longstreet's corps came upon the ground between the hours of 10 A. M. and 2 P. M. That they took no serious part in the action in the afternoon was owing to the fact that Stuart, whose cavalry was charged with the protection of Longstreet's right, reported the presence of the federal troops in strong force in that quarter, threatening, as he supposed, Longstreet's extreme right. Lee therefore sent the bulk of Longstreet's command there, instead of sending them to the direct support of Jackson. This force, which prevented Lee from re-inforcing Jackson in the afternoon, was that of Porter.

But toward sun-down McDowell was ordered forward along the Warrenton turnpike, and had a sharp fight with the enemy. Hatch, who commanded the division, tells the story of this attack : " We were met by a force consisting of three brigades of infantry. These were supported by a large portion of the rebel forces, estimated by a prisoner who was taken at their rear at about 30,000 men, drawn up in successive lines extending a mile and a half to the rear." (*Pope's Rep.* 177). The result was that Hatch was driven back. These three brigades, as will be seen by examining the confederate reports of Lee, Longstreet, and Hood (*Reb. Rec.* IX, 277, 570, 631), were the two of Hood and the one of Evans; as well as the supporting brigades, all belonged to Longstreet's corps. But they were only a part of it, for Longstreet's line stretched southward beyond the Manasses Railroad, out-flanking Porter.

Thus the entire "main body" of the confederate army was certainly within three hours' march at the very moment when Pope in his joint order placed them at a distance of thirty-six to forty-eight hours; they were on the field when he wrote the peremptory order to Porter to advance to the attack; they were preparing to attack Pope at the very hour when this order was received by Porter. (*Ibid* 633). Fully 40,000 strong, they occupied mainly the very position which Pope supposed to be empty, to which Porter, with 10,000 or 12,000 at most, was directed to march in order to fall upon Jackson's right and rear. Porter's prescribed line of march would have brought him upon the very centre of this force, strongly posted and greatly outnumbering him. The presence of this force, known to Porter, and wholly unsuspected by Pope, so changed all the conditions upon which the order was based, as to render its execution wholly impracticable; and therefore he would not have been justified in executing this order even had it reached him in time to have made a decided movement practicable, for he must have known that the order was given in utter ignorance of the actual position of affairs. Forty thousand and more men, of whose presence his Commanding-General knew nothing, stood in the way of his executing an order, to carry out which he had but a quarter as many.

The facts which I have adduced, each one of which is proven by evidence which seems to be of unquestioned authority, seem to me to show:

1. That in respect to the order of the 28th, Porter obeyed it in substance; and that in the apparent deviation from its terms, by commencing his march at three o'clock instead of one o'clock in the morning, he did not exceed the limits of the discretion vested in the commander of a corps; and that his course was

advised and approved by officers, than whom none in our army, then and since, stood higher in respect to zeal and courage.

2. That, in respect to the joint order of the 29th, ample discretion was, by the very terms of the order, given both to Porter and to McDowell, to decide whether it should be carried out ; and that in the action under this authority both were fully justifiable.

3. That in failing to comply with the order of 4.30 o'clock, Porter was justifiable on the ground that it would not have been given had his commanding officer been aware of the real circumstances of the case ; and that the attempt to execute it, had there been time, would have involved not merely failure, but the annihilation of his corps, and probably the destruction of the army of which it formed a part.

4. That, therefore, the court-martial should have honorably acquitted Porter upon both charges, and all the specifications under which he was arraigned.

Here, as far as the court-martial and its finding are concerned, the case properly ends. But the charges, as preferred, contained another specification, assuming that Porter, on the 30th of August :

Having received a lawful order from his superior officer, Major-General John Pope, to engage the enemy's lines and to carry a position near their centre, and to take an annoying battery there posted, did proceed in the execution of that order with unnecessary slowness, and by delay gave the enemy opportunities to watch and know his movements and to prepare to meet his attack, and did finally so feebly fall upon the enemy's lines as to make little impression upon the same, and did fall back and draw away his forces unnecessarily, and without making any of the great personal efforts to rally his troops or to keep their lines, or to inspire his troops to meet the sacrifices and to make the resistance demanded by the importance of his position, and the momentous consequences and disasters of a retreat at so critical a juncture of the day. (*Court-Martial*, 9.)

This charge was indeed withdrawn, the Judge-Advocate declining to attempt to prove it. [Though this specification was withdrawn by Judge-Advocate Holt, no evidence of the fact appears in the order promulgating the finding of the court. No such order was given me, nor any order other than that quoted by Dr. Guernsey, "*to pursue the enemy in his retreat, and press him vigorously during the whole day.*" That enemy was known at the time to be strongly posted in our front, and anxiously wishing an attack by us.—F. J. P.] And so the accused was shut out from any attempt to rebut it. But it stands upon record as having been preferred, and General Pope brings it in substance in his report (p. 24), and in his testimony before the court. I deem it right, therefore, to touch upon the transactions of August 30, the last day of the series of battles known in history as "the second Bull Run," or "the second Manassas," or, more properly, "the Battles of Groveton." I shall speak of them only in so far as they bear upon the part taken by Porter in that disastrous battle.

On the morning of the 30th, Porter, in obedience to an order from Pope, came upon the battle-field. At daylight, Pope had received intelligence which made him "feel discouraged and nearly hopeless of any successful issue to the operations with which he was charged." (*Report*, 23.) But soon after, he wrote to the General-in-Chief that he had won a victory over the "combined force" of the enemy. He had just been told that the enemy were in full retreat, and he was going to the front to see. He was convinced that this was true. "McDowell and Heintzelman, who had reconnoitered the positions held by the enemy's left on the evening of the 29th, reported that these positions had been evacuated, and that there was every indication that he was retreating in the direction of Gainesville." (*Pope's Rep.* 22.)

Never was there a more grave mistake. Lee, who had come up on the previous day, and assumed the control of all the operations on the field, had merely withdrawn Jackson's extreme left a little ; and during the morning had swung Longstreet's corps around directly from, instead of towards Gainesville. (*Reb. Rec.* IX, 636). The confederate right, which on the day before had run pretty nearly in a line with its left, now formed almost a right angle with it. Its shape was that of an open V reversed thus Λ. Pope's entire effective force on that morning, as given by himself, (Report 23), was 40,000 men. Lee's, making allowances for losses in action and on the march, was fully 60,000 exclusive of cavalry.

Pope, although, as he himself says, aware that " by twelve or one o'clock in the day we were confronted by forces greatly superior to our own, and these forces were being every moment largely increased by fresh arrivals of the enemy from the direction of Thoroughfare Gap" (*Pope's Rep.* 24), resolved to attack, or, as his order of twelve o'clock states, to " pursue the enemy," whom he knew to be advancing instead of retreating.

" The following forces," says the order from Pope (which is to be found in McDowell's report), " will be immediately thrown forward in pursuit of the enemy, and press him vigorously during the whole day. Major-General McDowell is assigned to the command of the pursuit. Major-General Porter's corps will push forward on the Warrenton turnpike, followed by the divisions of Brigadier-Generals King and Reynolds."

Of Porter's attack Pope says :

" It was neither vigorous nor persistent and his troops soon retired in considerable confusion.   *   *   Porter's forces were rallied and brought to a halt as they were retiring to the rear. As soon as they could be used I pushed them forward to support our left, and they there rendered most distinguished service, especially the brigade of regulars under Colonel Buchanan." (*Pope's Rep.*, 24).

A few brief extracts from the reports of commanders of Porter's corps, who took part in this action, will show the true character of this "feeble attack."

General Sykes, after describing the strong and sheltered positions of the enemy, says :

" About 4 P. M. I was ordered to support an attack to be made by General Butterfield. This attack was based upon the supposition that the enemy was in full retreat—so announced in the orders of General Pope. Porter's army corps was to be the centre of operations.   *   *   *   Butterfield's attack *was gallantly made and gallantly maintained* until his troops were torn to pieces. My first brigade, under Colonel R. C. Buchanan, moved to his aid, relieved him, and became furiously engaged. The enemy, posted in a railroad excavation, was as secure as earthen embankments could make him, and as our troops emerged from the woods they were met by withering volleys that decimated their ranks. Their own fire was almost harmless against a sheltered foe. The enemy, seeing the failure, and that one weak point lay on my left, in front of

Warren, poured on his weak command, under cover of the forest, a mass of infantry that enveloped, almost destroyed him. It became necessary to retire from the ground we occupied. Buchanan's and Chapman's brigades did go in columns of regiments, in line of battle under a severe artillery fire, and never wavered. * * The enemy continuing to outflank our left, Buchanan was ordered to the support of our forces engaged in that direction, maintained a gallant and bloody conflict with the foe until, outnumbered and badly crippled, I directed him to retire. Chapman, thrown in previous to Buchanan, fighting desperately for three-quarters of an hour, was also ordered to retire. * * * * After my command reunited, I received orders to move on to Centreville, and reached there at midnight, intact and in excellent order." (*Sykes, in Pope's Rep.*, 156-148).

I do not find any report by Butterfield of his attack; but the foregoing, from Sykes, proves the gallantry with which it was made. Warren also speaks in similar terms. He says:

As soon as General Butterfield's brigade advanced up the hill there was a great commotion among the rebel forces, and the whole side of the hill and edges of the woods swarmed with men before unseen. * * * After making a most desperate and hopeless fight, General Butterfield's troops fell back and the enemy immediately formed and advanced. (*Warren, in Pope's Rep.* 150.)

Of the gallantry of Warren's brigade, it is sufficient to say that of his two regiments, numbering but 1,000 men, 431 were killed or wounded. All the foregoing belonged to Porter's corps. King's division was also under Porter's command, and was no less prominent in the attack. Hatch, who now commanded this division, says:

Porter directed me to post the division on the right of his own troops, and to make the attack simultaneously with himself. At the word given by General Porter, the division advanced, with an interval of fifty yards between the lines. The enemy were very strongly posted behind an old dis-used railroad embankment, where, according to their own statement, they had been awaiting us for two days. * * * The contest for the possession of this embankment was most desperate. The troops on both sides fought with the most determined courage, and I doubt not the conflict at this point was one of the most bloody of the whole war.

The confederate official reports are equally direct and explicit as to the vigor with which this attack by Porter was made. Thus, General Lee says:

About 3 P. M. the enemy, having massed his troops in front of General Jackson, advanced against his position in strong force. His front line pressed forward until engaged at close quarters by Jackson's troops, when its progress was checked, and a fierce struggle ensued. A second and third line of great strength moved up to support the first, but in doing so came within easy range of a position a little in advance of Longstreet's left. (*Reb. Rec.* IX. 277.)

The "lines" thus mentioned were Porter's, for those were the only troops opposed to Jackson's right and Longstreet's left. Longstreet says:

Just after reaching my first line, I received a message for re-inforcements for General Jackson, who was said to be severely pressed. From an eminence near by, one portion of the enemy's masses attacking General Jackson were immediately within my view, and in easy range of batteries in that position. It gave me an advantage that I had not expected to have, and I made haste to use it. (*Ibid*, 571.)

The statement that the troops which were pressing Jackson were within view from Longstreets left, and within range of his batteries, shows that they were Porter's, for his were the only ones in such a position. Hood (*Ibid*, 633), says: "The battle was commenced by a *most vigorous* attack by the enemy upon the right of General Jackson." _Jackson says of this part of the engagement:

About 4 o'clock in the evening the federal infantry advanced in several lines, first engaging the *right*, but soon extending its attack to the centre and left. As one line was repulsed another took its place, and pressed forward as if determined, by force of numbers and fury of assault, to drive us from our positions. So *impetuous and well-sustained* were these onsets as to induce me to send to the commanding general for re-enforcements; but the timely and gallant advance of General Longstreet on the right, relieved my troops from the pressure. As Longstreet pressed

4

upon the right, the federal advance was checked, and soon a general advance of my whole line was ordered.

The vigor and persistency of an attack may, in a measure at least, be estimated from the loss suffered and inflicted. Porter's own corps numbered that morning, according to Pope, 7,000 men. It lost in this action 2,171 men, of whom 333 are put down as killed, 1,323 wounded, 518 missing; but as the field remained in possession of the enemy, many of those returned merely as "missing" were undoubtedly killed. The losses in King's division, which also attacked under Porter, were heavy; but I find no report of the numbers.

So much for the attack by Porter, which Pope, in contradiction to all who bore part in it on either side, declares to have been "neither vigorous nor persistent;" and which the abandoned charge before the court-martial characterizes still more severely. No wonder that the Judge-Advocate, whom no one will accuse of doing his duty negligently in this trial, abandoned this charge. I think I have shown that on the 30th of August, at Groveton, Fitz John Porter's conduct was worthy of the general who, on the 27th of June, fought the battle of Cold Harbor, and on the 1st of July won, according to McClellan, the chief honors at Malvern Hill.

There was much matter introduced upon the trial, which should not have influenced the finding of the court. It was apparent from the evidence that there was an unpleasant state of feeling between the Army of the Potomac and that of Virginia. Pope, in his general order upon assuming the command, had sneered at the manner in which the war had been conducted at the East. The Eastern officers had little confidence in Pope's military capacity. Porter certainly shared in this distrust; but there is no evidence that this feeling was expressed in an improper manner, or that it in the least interfered with his military conduct while under Pope's command.

Again, it is evident that Porter was warmly attached, both personally and professionally, to General McClellan. But no one will say that this feeling was other than praiseworthy. The student of history, who investigates some subsequent campaigns, will find abundant reason to regret that other corps commanders had not shared in this feeling for the generals commanding.

The Judge-Advocate, indeed, in his "Review" addressed to

the President, dwelt at length upon what he supposed to be the "animus" of the accused. But, if my conclusions are well founded that there is no criminality, this must all be dismissed. Still, if any one wishes to investigate the question of criminal "animus," I am confident that he will be convinced, even from the evidence adduced, that the accusation rests upon no tangible proofs, and was unworthy of being mentioned by the Judge-Advocate.

It has been no part of my purpose to inquire how and why a court-martial came to a conclusion which, in my judgment, is so wholly contrary to fact and justice. But I think I have proved that a great wrong has been done. And for every legal wrong there is a legal remedy. It is due to the nation, as well as to Fitz John Porter, that the wrong be righted as far as it can now be done.

COFFINVILLE, MISS., *September* 23d, 1866.

F. J. PORTER, ESQ., *New York City.*

SIR :—Your letter of the 7th inst. reached me at this point a few days ago. I have no objections to the questions contained in your letter, if my answers are not to be made use of in the public prints, and should have no objection to that but for the peculiar position which I now occupy. So far as I am able to do so I shall answer your questions, relying upon your discretion in the use you may make of the matter.

Ans. 1st. My command arrived within supporting distance of Jackson's command about 9 A. M., 29 August, near Groveton.

2d. Do not remember the time at which I heard that my right was threatened. But remember to have moved a column to my right to meet such threatening force, or rather to have moved a column to re-inforce my right.

3d. My command was deployed in double line, for attack, between 10 A. M. and 12 P. M., on the 29th, extending from Jackson's right across Turnpike and Manasses Gap R. R. Do not remember definitely the strength, but all of my command proper was up. R. H. Anderson arrived that night with three or four brigades, and was then assigned to my command.

4th. My command was ready to receive any attack after 11 o'clock A. M. ; and *we all were particularly anxious to bring on the battle after* 12 *M.* ; General Lee more so than the rest.

5th. My recollection of the ground on my right is that artillery could not be handled on it, and that infantry could not have been handled so as to make a formidable attack.

6th. If you had attacked any time after 12 M., it seems to me that we surely would have destroyed your army. That is, if you had attacked with less than twenty-five thousand men.

When I return to New Orleans I may be able to furnish more satisfactory information than I can at this distance from my papers, etc.

I am sir, very respectfully,

Your obedient servant,

J. LONGSTREET.

———— ◄► • ————

NEW YORK, *October* 11, 1866.

GEN. F. J. PORTER, *New York*.

GENERAL:—Your letter of yesterday has been received and read, and your quessions propounded in it will be answered fully and cheerfully, and with all the truth possible at this time—more than four years after the date of the incidents referred to.

In reply to your *first question*, I will state my command left Hopewell Gap early on the morning of the 29th of August, 1862, and continued its march rapidly till the other portion of Longstreet's command was encountered marching on the road from Thoroughfare Gap to Gainesville. My troops halted till the others had passed, and then followed closely in the rear. The halt was for a short time, as the troops had been passing for some time. The time of junction of my command with the other portions of Longstreet's command, I gave in my report of second Manasses, at 9:30 A. M. It is also stated that after advancing some three miles beyond Gainesville, my brigades were formed in line of battle on the left of the Pike, and at right angles to it, and advanced near a mile and halted, the enemy being in our front. Several of our batteries were in position on the left of the Pike firing at the enemy, and his batteries replying, most of the balls and shells falling short of my command, which was about 1000 yards in rear of the artillery.

Second question. I think it was near 2 P. M. when my command halted in rear of our batteries, and this halt was made, I should say, one and one-half miles short of Groveton, or a little over this distance. Other portions of Longstreet's command were in my front on both sides of the Pike. I was in rear to support.

Third question. In my report I stated that at 4:30 or 5 P. M., my brigades were moved across to the right of the Pike a mile or more to the Manasses Gap railroad. Here they were formed some 1000 yards in rear of other troops (D. R. Jones), and to meet a supposed movement of the enemy on this part of the field.

Fourth question. I did not move up to our front lines, and so had no knowledge from a close inspection of the ground in front, but I have been from the Pike near Groveton on horseback, both to Manasses Junction and Bristoe Station, in the autumn of 1861, and remember the general features of the country, and should say it would have been very difficult, and attended with much delay, to have taken infantry and artillery over that country.

Fifth question. As stated in answer to second question, I was in rear as a support, and can't be precise as to either the time of formation on the south side of the Pike, or as to the brigades that were formed on that side. The troops, I think, were two brigades under D. R. Jones, Evans and three other of Longstreet's brigades, including, also, Hood's Texas brigade.

Sixth question. I should think that by 11 A. M., had you attacked the troops on the Pike, and to the right (our right) of the Pike, you would probably have been repulsed; 10,000 troops would have been rather a light body for an attack at that point, for our side would have been increased certainly and rapidly until the rear (my command) had come up.

With reference to the last paragraph of your letter, in which reference is made to evidence given by three officers on your trial, to the effect that none of Longstreet's forces were in your front, or in support of Jackson's right before sundown, I will state that I was the last to form on the right of the Pike, and that I formed at the time I stated above, and when I formed on the right of the Pike there was but one brigade on Longstreet's left—Jones' brigade, Hood's division.

I have read Dr. Guernsey's article in the World, and on such points as I have knowledge of, regard it as quite accurate and just. The strength of our brigades are over estimated, I think. In my three, two had about *sixteen hundred* muskets, and the other about twenty-two hundred or twenty-three hundred. The distance from Hopewell Gap to Gainesville was, I think, more than five miles. Thoroughfare Gap, I should say, was also more than that distance. It is, however, only my opinion, formed by marching over the ground but once.

The attack made on Jackson's right on the 30th was made with great vigor by the leading column. So much as I saw was creditable in the extreme to the attacking column. The supports to the part of your attacking column that I saw were broken by a close and well directed artillery fire.

Very truly, &c.,

C. M. WILCOX.

BALTIMORE, *May* 30*th*, 1869.

GEN. FITZ JOHN PORTER, *New York.*

GENERAL:—I received your message, through Gen. Field about 1 P. M. to-day, and am sorry that you need the information so soon, as I have to leave home at 4 P. M. to be absent a few days, and will not, therefore, be able to state the force of the confederate army at the second Manassas as accurately as I might do with a little more time.

The infantry of Jackson was in three divisions—Jackson's Division, Ewell's, under Lawton (after 28th), and A. P. Hill's.

Longstreet arrived on the morning of the 29th August with D. R. Jones' division of three brigades, Hood with two brigades, Evans one, Wilcox three, Kemper three. Jackson was reduced by hard marching and fighting before the 29th, and according to the best recollection I have now, his effective infantry on the 29th was about twenty thousand. Longstreet had, as you will see, twelve brigades of infantry on the 29th. I think his effective present was probably not less than thirty thousand, as some of the brigades were pretty full.

There were about two brigades of cavalry, and, I think, about the ordinary complement of artillery to such an infantry force as we had; perhaps a little less than we generally used.

I think it safe to say our total effective present was:

Longstreet, infantry,............................... 30,000
Jackson,   "   20,000
Artillery for both,................................. 4,000
Cavalry, ... 2,500

The cavalry had been greatly reduced by hard service before we got to Manassas.

The corps organization had not then been completed.

D. H. Hill was en route from Richmond, as also was McLaws.

R. H. Anderson came up early in the afternoon of the 29th, in time to have re-inforced Longstreet, and was held in reserve. He had about 7,000.

The arrival of D. H. Hill's and McLaw's divisions after the battle of the 30th, both of which were large, and had seen no service since the battles around Richmond, about restored our effective strength.

I can speak with some definiteness as to the time of Longstreet's arrival on the 29th, though I cannot fix the exact hour. But I do know that his troops came into the turnpike road from the direction of Thoroughfare Gap, striking the turnpike near Gainesville. As they came up to the position occupied by Jackson, some of them were at first advanced to take position on his right, which rested near the turnpike, and which the federal troops appeared to be endeavoring to turn. The appearance of Longstreet's column caused an immediate change in Gen. Pope's dispositions, and his left was drawn back, so as to bring his line nearly or quite at right angles to the road. Longstreet's troops were then pushed forward as they reached the ground, and formed on Jackson's right, extending our line at right angles to and east of the turnpike. Most of Longstreet's troops had reached or were reaching their position, when Stuart, who was on our right, reported the approach of a force from the direction of Manassas, or rather by the road leading by our flank to Manassas, and by the other towards Bristoe. As soon as this report had been received, General Lee sent D. R. Jones' division, not yet in line, to the right, recalled part of Longstreet's troops, already formed or forming on the right of the road, and moved them around to support Jones. The result was that the greater part of Longstreet's command changed front from north to east, and remained fronting the troops approaching from Manassas until some time in the afternoon (some of them until night). Those troops, I understood afterwards, were yours, and I am positive that they approached the field after Longstreet's arrival, and that the disposition of his troops had to be changed to meet them, as I have above described. I cannot give the hour, because I did not come from Thoroughfare Gap with the column. I slept the night before at a house west of the Gap, had a chill in the night, and was not ready to go with General Lee, who left about sunrise, but followed him as soon as the fever following the chill subsided. I passed the Gap certainly as early as 8 A. M., and took the road through Haymarket to Gainesville. The road was clear of troops, nor did I come up with any until I reached the turnpike, where I found some halted on each side of the road, those at the head of the column at that time moving to occupy the first position as above described.

If I can be of any assistance to you in ascertaining the truth, I shall be pleased to do so. I was an eye witness of the circumstances that were afterwards made the ground of charges against you, and do but repeat the sentiment of every officer in our army who was present, when I say that those circumstances were not truly presented before the Court.

> Very respectfully,
>
> Your obedient servant,
>
> CHARLES MARSHALL.

NEW YORK, *September* 16, 1867.

GENERAL U. S. GRANT, *Secretary of War.*

GENERAL:—I am to-day in receipt of a copy of a report sent to me by order of the President of the United States, endorsed upon my application for a Board to re-examine the proceedings in my case.

From the Report to the President I understand that you desire " I should demonstrate to the satisfaction of the authorities my ability to controvert by new evidence the testimony on which I was convicted."

I presume an outline of the testimony I propose to adduce before the Board to be appointed, is all that you either desire at my hands at this time, or your time will permit you to investigate.

In this view of the case I respectfully beg leave to submit, that :

Under the charge of violating the Ninth Article of War, in not marching at one o'clock instead of three o'clock on the night of the 27th of August, 1862, upon which I was adjudged guilty, I propose to show by General Patrick, Colonel H. C. Ransom— a member of Pope's Staff at the time—and others, that it was impossible to have made an effective march that night at an earlier hour, and that when I moved no delay attributable to me was had.

Under the charge of failing on the 29th of August, 1862,

" To push forward my forces on the enemy's flank and rear, etc., as well as that I did retreat from advancing forces of the enemy, without any attempt to engage them, or to aid the troops already fighting greatly superior numbers, etc.," and that the other portion of the army " were relying on the flank attack I was then ordered to make to secure a decisive victory, and to capture the enemy's army, a result which must have followed from said flank attack had it been made, etc."

In as much as the possibility of such action by me as he desired at any period within hours of the time which General Pope considered available, depends altogether upon the *time* in the afternoon at which the order was received by me, or the time when action under that order, or the discretion allowed me, would have been of service, I propose to show by the testimony of Generals Longstreet, Wilcox and others, whose letters I place in your hands for perusal, that at no time for hours anterior to the writing of General Pope's order, was there a possibility of my making the movement directed by him, except with the certainty of annihilation of my command; inasmuch as by the testimony of these and other confederate officers, it is shown that the corps of Longstreet, numbering not less than 30,000 men (my own command being less than 11,000 men) was in my front hours before the order of General Pope to me was even penned; and,

That the position, which was the only tenable one left to me under the circumstances, did accomplish all and more than the strict fulfillment of General Pope's order contemplated, in that I held (as shown by Generals Longstreet and Wilcox's letters before referred to) a large body of the enemy in my front that else would have engaged other portions of our army, already fully employed as has been shown.

The reports of the Army of Northern Virginia—since published in the "Rebellion Record," volume 9—all corroborate the position taken by me (upon information had at that time), as not only correct, but, as General Longstreet now says, "Had you attacked me at any time after 12 M., we surely would have destroyed your army, if you had attacked with less than 25,000 men."

Making little or no reference to my official conduct during the years preceding the period immediately under consideration, I also propose to show that my subsequent conduct, and that of the troops under my command—that is, on the 30th of August, the day following the one wherein it is alleged General Pope's orders were disobeyed—was of such a character as to prove, in the most conclusive manner, my energy and fidelity.

I am the more anxious to do this, as the court did not deem

the testimony at the time admissible—the specification having been withdrawn under which I had hoped to do so.

I shall have the testimony of Generals Butterfield, Sykes, and others in my behalf.

I may have occasion to revert to some of the testimony taken before the previous court in the course of the re-investigation, and with the light thrown upon many matters by the close of the war, thus give an opportunity for those who desire to revise their testimony.

Evidence more or less important on other points is at hand, but too tedious to present for your consideration at this time. I propose to bring it forward from time to time before the Board, as circumstances may require.

I am, General, with high respect,

Your obedient servant,

FITZ JOHN PORTER.

HEAD QUARTERS THIRD MILITARY DISTRICT, }
ATLANTA, GEORGIA, *Sept.* 16*th*, 1867. }

GENERAL U. S. GRANT, *Washington City:*

GENERAL,—As I am one of the principal parties concerned in the case of Fitz John Porter, and as I learn that he is in Washington City seeking a re-opening of his case, on the ground that he has come into possession of testimony since the close of the war which has an important bearing on the subject, and as I suppose it is not unlikely that a commission may be ordered to examine that testimony and report upon it, I consider it my duty, as well as my right, respectfully to submit to your attention, or that of any commission that may be ordered, the following remarks for such consideration as they merit.

It is unnecessary to set out here in detail the charges and specifications on which Fitz John Porter was tried and convicted, but I respectfully ask to submit a few remarks upon them, merely to call attention to the points of the case established by testimony and uncontroverted by the defence. The only answer made by the defence to the facts established is in the way of explanation or excuse.

To the first charge and first specification (the disobedience of orders being admitted by defence), the answer is, the night was dark, and there was danger of delay and straggling in executing the order for the march; but it will be noticed, and I ask especial attention to this fact, that no attempt was even made to obey the order. It was also established in the testimony on the subject that the whole of McDowell's and Sigel's corps marched nearly all night that same night on a march, but five or six miles north of Porter's corps, and that during the whole night messengers were passing between my head quarters, to which Porter was ordered, and his own and other corps of the army.

·How valid such an excuse as darkness is in the face of a positive order setting forth that the presence of his corps "was necessary on all accounts," I leave to your judgment; especially in the light of the fact that not even an attempt was made under such pressing orders and necessities to bring the corps forward. The whole of the circumstances on this point are fully set forth in the testimony.

Although the general plea of "not guilty" was made by the defence to all charges and specifications, yet it was not disputed that the orders set forth in specifications to the charges were received. Neither (except in the case of the joint order to McDowell and Porter) is it claimed that the orders were obeyed. Substantially the details set forth in all the specifications except the fourth and fifth specifications of the first charge, and the fourth specification of the second charge remain undisputed, except as to certain phrases and words and the general impression conveyed. The only defence set up was in the way of excuse, and comprises two points:

1st. That the ground in front of Porter's corps was difficult, and that the road on which he was marching was occupied by the right wing of the enemy, who extended across it.

2d. That the enemy was believed to be in heavy force, and that an attack would have been unsuccessful.

To the first of these points it is only necessary to say that the difficulty of ground, even if it existed, is no excuse for failing to obey an order, and particularly for failing to try to obey it.

The fact established in the testimony that the enemy next day moved over this very ground and attacked our left, is sufficient answer as to difficulty of ground, should such a pretext be thought to have any weight.

In relation to the force of the enemy in front of Porter, I beg leave respectfully to submit that that question has no bearing on the subject. Whether there were five thousand or fifty thousand of the enemy confronting Porter is a matter not at all affecting the question of his conduct. A general battle was and had for hours been raging on Porter's right, and almost in his sight, certainly in his hearing. He had in his command nearly a third of the whole Union army. His corps had been re-inforced by Piatt's Brigade, and numbered quite 12,000 men,

One of his divisions contained nearly the whole of the regular army.

It was abundantly supplied with artillery, and was altogether the most effective corps on the field. It had marched only three or four miles, and was therefore by far the freshest corps in the entire army. Yet it did not fire a gun during the entire battle of the 29th of August, 1862, but lay on the ground with its arms stacked for seven hours of that battle without an attempt either to attack the enemy in front, or to come to the assistance of the other troops elsewhere engaged in deadly conflict, and who (as Porter himself says in his dispatch addressed to McDowell and King) he believed were being overpowered and driven from the field.

In the face of a positive order to attack he did not move, and when convinced from the sounds of the battle on his right, that that portion of the army was worsted, he retired from the field, not *towards* the army which needed his help, but in the opposite direction, although the road was open to him, and messengers and orderlies were passing to and fro. These are facts established by the testimony, and undisputed by the defence. If, in a general battle, a corps or a division commander, receiving a positive order to attack a portion of the enemy's line, has the right to disobey this order on the ground that he does not believe the attack would be successful, I cannot see how any combinations can be made by the commanding-General, or how he can expect that any of his orders will be obeyed. How can a corps commander know that the General-in-chief expects his attack to be successful? How can he know that he is not ordered to attack a particular point of the enemy's line, in order that sufficient force to resist his attack may be withdrawn from other points to render an assault elsewhere successful? How can he know that his attack is not intended to prevent the enemy's troops in front of him from re-inforcing other parts of their line upon which an attack is being made? The effect of an attack by Porter, even had he been repulsed, at any time from mid-day to eight o'clock, on the evening of the 29th of August, 1862, is clearly set forth in General McDowell's testimony in this case. Had Sherman failed to attack the enemy's right at Chattanooga, on the ground that the enemy was in strong force, and he would be repulsed (as indeed, was the fact) what would have become of Hooker—what, indeed, of the entire victory at Chattanooga ? In truth, I feel ashamed to offer any argument to military men on such a matter. They are potent, and as well recognized as the first principles of discipline.

I say, then, that whether the enemy's force in front of Porter was great or small, it makes not the slightest excuse for his not obeying his orders, nor can any excuse be found, even admitting the above to be one, for an officer who not only disobeys an order to attack but absolutely keeps a larger effective force out of action anywhere during a whole day of battle in his presence. If he was afraid to attack in his front, why did he not bring his corps to the aid of the rest of the army which he says himself (in his despatch to McDowell and King) he believes was being worsted ? Why above all did he march *away from* instead of towards the Union Army ?

The amount of the enemy's force in front of him, I need not farther say, has no bearing upon the subject, since he knew not for what purpose an attack was ordered; but it so happens in this case that testimony on that point, unimportant and irrelevant as it is, is at hand. I presume it will be admitted that the best authority as to the amount of the enemy's force in front of Porter on the 29th August, 1862, is the report of the officer in command of the enemy confronting him on that day.

This officer was General J. E. B. Stuart, of the rebel army. He is now dead, but fortunately his report is to be found in the volume of rebel reports of the campaign, published by the rebel congress. Copies of these published reports are in the hands of the Government, and easily accessible.

He (General Stuart) reports that he commanded on Jackson's right on the 29th August, 1862, with a ridiculously small force of cavalry and some small guns ; that he saw a heavy force, which he estimated at 20,000 men, marching upon Jackson's flank; that he was made very uneasy, and sent back word to Jackson ; that he disposed of his small cavalry force so as to make as great a display as possible, and made thirty or forty of his men cut brush and gallop up and down the Warrenton turnpike in his rear, so as to make a great dust, and give the impression that heavy forces were on that road ; that his ruse was successful, and that the enemy halted and then fell back.

He further states that this force was Fitz John Porter's corps.

I do not pretend to quote literally, but this report can easily be had, and the exact words ascertained. Further than this, Longstreet himself reports of his own corps, the strength of which can be easily ascertained, that he had made forced marches for several days before, and a very long and hard forced march on that day, fighting part of the time with Rickett's division.

It is certain his corps was in little condition, when it arrived on the field, to contend with Porter's, which, nearly, if not quite, of equal strength, was perfectly fresh, and contained the best troops of the army. To say at this day, that Longstreet's wearied and almost broken-down corps was able to overpower the fifth corps of our army, is the bitterest commentary upon that corps its worst enemy could make, and, I have no doubt, is utterly groundless. It would indeed be remarkable, if overpowering forces of the enemy were all day in front of Porter, that he was not attacked by them—as astonishing as his own failure to attack.

I cite these facts as to the force of the enemy in front of Porter merely as they seem to be interesting, and not because they have any bearing whatever upon Porter's guilt or innocence. That was determined upon other grounds, which no military man will fail to recognize.

I beg attention, however, to what will, I think, very fully explain Porter's conduct.

Despatches sent from him to Burnside, sent before and after he joined me, and intended, as he says himself, for McClellan, are to be found on the records of the court-martial. They indicate a state of mind, and a hostility and bitterness, I will venture to say, unparalleled under such circumstances. They present the grossest and most outrageous violation of discipline and military propriety, to say nothing of ordinary good manners, which can be found on any official record in this country.

That a subordinate officer, in face of the enemy, without knowledge of the number or disposition either of the enemy's forces or our own, and in the midst of a deadly conflict, upon which the very existence of the government and the lives of thousands of patriotic men were at stake, could write such despatches almost surpasses belief. As I said, it indicates a state of mind capable of anything, and these despatches themselves furnish the completest explanation of Porter's conduct which can ever be given.

I take it for granted, as the general facts set forth in the specification of the charges against Porter were and are completely proved, that the testimony he now brings forward upon which to base a re-opening of his case, is simply testimony as to the amount of the enemy's force in front of him on the 29th August, 1862.

I respectfully submit that such testimony, even if strictly true, has no bearing upon the findings and sentence of the court-martial in his case, and furnishes no reason whatever for re-opening the case.

I am, General,

very respectfully,

Your obedient servant,

JNO. POPE,
Bvt-Maj-Gen., U. S. A.

———

NEW YORK, *October 16th*, 1867.

To His Excellency, ANDREW JOHNSON,
President of the United States.

SIR:—I have been permitted to read a communication from Major-General John Pope to General Grant, Secretary of War, in which the former asserts himself to be "one of the principal parties concerned" in my case, and considers it his duty, as well as his right, to enter his protest against the appeal for a re-examination of the proceedings which Senators Wilson, Sherman, Harris and Foster, Governor Curtin, General Banks, Hon. Horace Greeley and other distinguished citizens, have in my behalf asked at your hands.

In my application to you for a re-examination of the charges against me, I supposed I had avoided every expression which could offer embarassment to any gentleman connected with the prosecution who felt disposed to revise testimony given by him on the trial, by the light of newly discovered evidence. In what I have done to vindicate my good name everything has been open and in the light of day. I have not endeavored to create public opinion or control it. I have not asked for congressional or any other final action in advance of facts ascertained under the forms and sanction of military judicature. I have not asked for the appointment of an inferior commission, but have urged the selection of a Board of Officers so high in rank and in public esteem, that its decision would everywhere carry conviction of the soundness thereof. You are aware that so careful have I been to exclude all possibility of partisan prejudice or political emotion, that I suggested that my application be referred to General Grant for report and action thereunder. Against this disposition of my case Major General Pope alone protests. He has no willingness to avail himself of the opportunity offered to assist in the proposed inquiry for the ascertainment of truth, but rises up as an accuser in a case in which, at one time, he only claimed to be an unwilling witness.

Distinguished Senators and upright citizens, familiar with the whole field of military operations during the late war, represent to the President that evidence unattainable at the former trial, pertinent to the issues involved, and now within easy access, is sufficient to warrant the appointment of a commission "to examine this evidence and ascertain whether injustice has not been done?" but Major-General Pope protests against being again required to submit his statements and allegations to such a test. Will your Excellency permit me to so far trespass upon your time as to place on record a few suggestions in answer to the volunteered communication of Major-General Pope, which, while they serve to show the errors amid which that officer still wanders, may perchance indicate to you the importance of the newly discovered evidence now accessible?

The main points contained in General Pope's communication may be summed up as follows:

1st. That no attempt was made to execute the order of 6.30 P. M., of August 27th, 1862, to march at one o'clock at night, &c.

Answer. I shall show by recorded testimony, to which I propose to materially add, that I attempted and did execute the order as far as practicable, the only modification being a change in the hour of march from one to three o'clock. This change was induced by the remonstrance of officers next to me in command, whose judgment, skill, and bravery can never justly be called in question. They urged that literal compliance was impossible, and would, if attempted, render my corps wholly unfit for the additional service specified for that morning ; my troops then being without food, wearied by long, forced, and unceasing marches. It was also urged and agreed that even at three o'clock, when the troops did move, no substantial progress could be made till increasing light permitted.

2nd. That it is established in testimony that both McDowell and Sigel's corps marched nearly all that night (August 27th), a few miles north of my corps.

Answer. In the spirit in which this allegation is presented by

General Pope, he is in error, for I shall establish by new testimony that—

The turnpike over which these corps were directed to march that night was of a much better character than the country road my command was to traverse, and that—

During the short time these corps were marching, the same difficulties were experienced as by my troops, and that no substantial gain or progress was made in the darkness; and also that—

Officers, some of them members of General Pope's staff, leaving my camp at midnight for Bristoe Station (my destination), were forced from the road by obstructions, and lost their way in the darkness, though conducted by an experienced guide, and did not reach General Pope till 8 A. M., on the 28th.

3*d.* "That it is not disputed General Pope's orders were received."

Answer. It *is* disputed that General Pope's orders were, in any case, *received within a reasonable period after they purported to have been issued.* It can be shown that all of General Pope's orders were delayed in the delivery; and it is proved by the testimony of General Sykes, Colonel Locke, Captains Montieth, Weld and others, that the order of 4.30 P. M. on 29th August, was not received by me till too late to execute.

4*th.* That the enemy did, on the 30th August, " pass over the ground claimed by me as impassable, and attack the left of our army."

Answer. The facts are that, although the enemy did, on the day succeeding that in question, *i. e.,* on the 30th of August, succeed in pushing some troops over a portion of the ground regarded impassable, in the immediate presence of an opposing force, still they were employed from early in the morning to 2 o'clock P. M., in doing that which even General Pope's own version allowed me less than three hours to accomplish; and there is the additional fact that no force of ours then opposed the enemy, whereas on the preceding day I was expected to traverse the same ground in much less time, overwhelmingly opposed:

That no artillery was taken by the enemy through or over that ground, and

That, as I shall prove by General Longstreet and others, the ground, by reason of its broken character, dense woods, &c., was not only impracticable for the handling of artillery, but also for the successful handling of infantry in any large body.

In a word, the testimony of Generals Reynolds and Morell, Colonel E. G. Marshall and others, as adduced heretofore, is completely established.

5th. "That a general battle was and had been raging on my right, and almost in my sight—certainly in my hearing—for hours; and that I had nearly a third of the whole Union Army under my command at that time, &c."

"That my troops did not fire a gun during the entire battle."

"That I did not attempt to assist troops elsewhere, though I had written Generals McDowell and King, I believed our forces were being overpowered and driven from the field, and

"That I believed the enemy's force in front of me was very heavy, and that therefore an attack would be unsuccessful."

Answer. I shall show that no general battle was in progress between noon and 5.30 P. M. that day (August 29th), and in addition to the testimony heretofore adduced, I will show by General Pope's official report, that between these hours no more than "heavy skirmishing" was had;

That so far from being within sight or sound of any heavy firing between these hours, the woods were so dense and the ground was of such a nature, that no sound of a general or any engagement, other than artillery firing at long range, reached me or my command;

That my troops, while but little engaged in action that day, held a position of the highest importance; for, as stated hereinafter, they were so disposed as to draw from before General Pope, and to keep the whole of Longstreet's larger forces in front of me, thereby securing all the good effects of a battle without its injuries.

I shall substantiate the evidence that I was held in my position by McDowell's orders, which, being reiterated, caused the recall of a division of my corps moving to attack, and that it was not judicious, nor admissable upon information in my possession, furnished from time to time by General McDowell and others, to at any time go to the assistance of General Pope; the belief, based on rumor, expressed in my note to Generals Mc-

Dowell and King, having been, as shown in the evidence, incorrect.

I shall substantiate the record that General McDowell was in command and present with me at the only time on the 29th August, before 6 P. M., when the sounds of battle (artillery only) were audible; that my command mainly was there, and remained during the whole day substantially in contact with the enemy; that General Pope's order to General McDowell and myself was issued on the erroneous supposition that " the whole force of the enemy would not arrive till to-morrow (the 30th) or next day;" that from prisoners then in my possession, belonging to Longstreet's corps, and from General Buford's letter to General Ricketts, shown to me by General McDowell, in connection with other information possessed by General Mc-Dowell, it was evident that we were then (twelve o'clock noon on the 29th) confronted by Longstreet's forces, and that the object of our combined movement had been frustrated; that, acting on this belief and on General Pope's instruction that " the troops must occupy a position from which they can reach Bull Run that night," General McDowell, exercising a discretion authorized in the order, directed me to remain on that ground, and did himself turn back and march away beyond support of me, with the divisions of King and Ricketts (over half our joint forces), to a point close to Bull Run, which he was several hours in reaching; and that, by thus withdrawing, he prevented all possibility of severing the connection of Longstreet with Jackson, which was the object of our combined movement.

I will also prove by what General Pope considers competent authority—General Longstreet himself—that I was correct both as to the greatly superior force in my front, and as to the probable effect of an attack by me.

I shall prove that Longstreet desired an attack, and considered it would have resulted, after McDowell's withdrawal, advantageously to himself, and as suggested that evening by me to General Pope, in serious disaster to my corps; and that the position taken by me, not only saved my corps, but in the most effective manner served the purposes of General Pope, by holding in check a force largely superior to may own, and drawing supports from the troops opposing General Pope.

6th. "That when convinced from the sounds of the battle on the right, that our army was being worsted, I marched *away* from giving assistance, and went in an opposite direction although; the road was open, and orderlies, &c., passing to and fro."

Answer. As I have said above, the opinion expressed in my note to Generals McDowell and King, proved incorrect, and was not acted upon, nor was it designed to be acted upon, as is shown in the note itself, till "I communicated with them."

I have shown, and will bring additional testimony to show, that at no time did I *march away from giving assistance,* or give any order tending to do so; but all day and all night of the 29th, till called away on the 30th by General Pope's orders, the largest portion of my command remained where General McDowell left it, and directed it to be, which was in almost immediate contact with the enemy, while the remainder was properly held, during the same time, massed in rear in support, prepared to go, if called or necessary, to General Pope's assistance, taking, as it was then, and had been all day, on the only practicable route, the same road taken by General McDowell and his troops, and by my command the following morning. It is true that General McDowell, in the exercise of his discretion, did march away with his command on the afternoon of the 29th August, whilst *my* troops did not march away till the next morning, *having alone confronted and held the enemy till that time,* and most fortunately, as I shall show by competent testimony, for our other forces.

I shall also show, on this point, that the orderlies passing back and forth, were mainly my messengers carrying information to and in vain seeking instructions from Generals McDowell and Pope, and that so far from bringing information that assistance was needed by General Pope, the reverse was the fact.

7th. "That the effect of an attack by me at any time between noon and eight o'clock of the evening of the 29th of August, even though repulsed, would have been most beneficial, and General McDowell's testimony before my court is referred to as endorsing this view of the case" and quoted to sustain General Pope's claim that "my withholding an attack between the hours of twelve and eight prevented the capture or destruction of Jackson on the 29th August."

Answer. General Pope apparently forgets that General Mc-Dowell expressed this as a "mere opinion," which is not "evidence," and that it was based upon the erroneous opinion that Jackson's forces alone confronted our army between these hours, and to the exclusion of official reports from his general officers, which should all have been, as some were, in his possession.

It is hardly necessary to state, in the light of facts now readily ascertainable, and, at the time, deemed unnecessary, adverse opinions from the best military sources can and will be given, completely nullifying this opinion of General McDowell, if still retained by him, showing at that time no such opinion was entertained by those who, having been in contact with the enemy, enjoyed far better opportunities of possessing correct information than either General McDowell or General Pope. It is true that General Pope telegraphed the War Department, and electrified the country by the information that "the enemy was retreating to the mountains;" but that assertion unhappily proved untrue, and, as is known, was based upon a total misconception of the enemy's forces and position.

8th. That even though the question of a largely superior force confronting me, were admissable, it is (General Pope claims) shown by the commanding-General of the enemy (J. E. B. Stuart, in his official report) to have been very small—"that he disposed of his small force—trailed brushes to cause dust and thus convey the idea of numbers, and that my corps halted and fell back."

Answer. I am, perhaps, saved the necessity of imputing to General Pope a want of veracity in this respect, inasmuch as he claims to quote General Stuart's report from memory.

Between his memory of the report, and the report itself, the difference will be best shown by reference to it, by which it will be seen,

That Longstreet's forces were on the field before my arrival.

That "the prolongation of my line of march would have passed through Stuart's position," "a very fine one for artillery," and "struck Longstreet in flank."

That he awaited my approach long enough to ascertain something of my strength, dragging brush, etc., to attempt to deceive me, notifying the commanding-General, "*then opposite me on the turnpike,*" that "*Longstreet's flank and rear* were seriously threatened, and of the importance of the ridge I held;" that immediately the brigades of Jenkins, Kemper, and D. R. Jones were sent, together with artillery, placed in position, and waited my advance, and,

That after exchanging a few shots with rifled pieces, this corps (mine) withdrew towards Manassas, "leaving artillery and supports to hold the position till night."

In explanation of this last paragraph, I shall show by the recorded testimony and confirmatory evidence, that it refers to the division of Morell, sent forward by me after General Mc-Dowell retired from that ground, and recalled to its former position under General McDowell's reiterated order, before any exchange of artillery shots. This division was then posted on its original ground (as Morell has testified) in a manner to invite attack, and was there held till daybreak the following morning.

In addition to the force at that time sent to General Stuart, a division was, later in the day, withdrawn from the support of Jackson and placed in my front, on the extreme right of Long-street's forces, "in case," says General Longstreet's official report, "of an attack against my right."

Thus it is proven by the enemy themselves that my action and the position retained by my corps drew from General Jackson's support a large force.

9th. "That Lonstreet himself reports that his corps had made large and forced marches, and also, on the day in question (August 29th), had made a forced march and fought Ricketts' division, and that my troops were fresh, and nearly or quite equal in numbers to Longstreet;" and

"That, if Longstreet's corps had so great a numerical superiority, it is remarkable he did not attack me."

Answer. A reference to General Longstreet's Report (volume 9, Rebellion Record, p. 570) shows the inaccuracy of this statement of General Pope. Not one word is written by General Longstreet as to his troops having made long and forced marches; and all references by Longstreet, Hood, and D. R. Jones (a small part only of the latter's division having engaged Ricketts) to the encounter with Ricketts' division, show that it was only "a spirited little engagement" (loss of twenty-five men), "heavy demonstrations and skirmishing" on Ricketts' side; and this all occurred on the 28th of August, some twenty hours prior to the events referred to.

General Longstreet's failure to attack my inferior forces has no pertinency, save to indicate that my troops were so disposed as to deceive him as to my real strength and purpose, and thus relieve General Pope from combatting an enemy already too great either in number or skill for him to successfully attack.

It will be proved, however, that the *desire* of General Longstreet was to invite attack, and that, had I fallen into this error, his position and strength were such, whatever the condition of his troops, that my command would probably have been destroyed.

10th. "That I did not even try to pass over the ground between me and the enemy on the 29th August, which I claimed as impassable, and also occupied by the right wing of the enemy."

Answer. I shall show that the movement to pass over that ground was thwarted by General McDowell's orders to me, and most fortunately it was so; and, also,

That even an effort to communicate by messengers failed, from the nature of the country and the occupation of it by the enemy.

Finally, General Pope assumes to explain the cause of what he terms my conduct in the matter, contained in the charges brought before the court.

In attempting this he but rehearses what was termed the "animus" of my alleged conduct, by the prosecution on the trial.

A few words in explanation of these dispatches, which seem to have highly incensed General Pope, may suffice for the present. They were confidential (though partly official) communications to General Burnside, whose tenure near Aquia Creek was dependant upon correct information of our movements and of those of the enemy. Made at his request, they became official by the anxious call of the President for just such information as I was giving of the Army, communication with which had been cut off, except by the channel I had, at great trouble, and in fear of disaster, established and maintained till eventually called, August 29th, by General Pope to Centreville. This point was nearer and on the direct road to

Alexandria, through which General Burnside would necessarily the soonest hear of us, and I so informed him.

They were *not* designed, as asserted by General Pope, for General McClellan, of whose position and relations to the army I knew nothing. In the haste of dispatch they were carelessly expressed. If they manifested confidence in General Mc-Clellan, and a distrust of General Pope's ability to conduct the campaign (as claimed by the prosecution), they but expressed the opinion pervading our Eastern armies.

Each dispatch covered one of General Pope's orders, and was designed to convey a correct impression of affairs, and to undo the effect of false reports. Should I be blamed if they show— as is now apparent—that General Pope at least misconceived the situation, and that I was better acquainted than he is willing to admit he was, with the position and movements of the contending forces and the wants of the army, and that forseeing the inevitable results of that campaign, I should have tried to provide against its disaster? Would I not have been justly held culpable had I, knowing the truth, failed to have expressed it, even without the call of the President, through General Burnside—and pointed out, as I did, the mode of guarding against the effects of misfortunes already brought upon us and others to come? Because I indicated the inevitable results of this campaign, General Pope unjustly claims I desired and worked for them.

I have, however, to state that the President, in person, thanked me for my despatches, as furnishing the only reliable information received at that time from the army, and as leading to the happiest results.

I believed, at the time of the trial, as I do now, that, if at the time and in the manner I desired, all my despatches had been permitted in evidence as well as the occasion of sending them, connected with the desire of the President to have just such information, this element—so delicate at all times to righteously use—probing and deciding upon, as it assumed to do, the secret thoughts and purposes of the human mind—that this element, my "*animus*," so potentially used against me, would have been completely foiled of its purpose, and this, too, without adducing n my behalf, as under such proceedings I should have had the right to do, an untarnished record both prior and subsequent to the unfortunate campaign of General Pope.

General Pope comments upon the duty of subordinate officers towards a General commanding; asks what confidence such an officer could have if his subordinates were at liberty to judge of his purposes or plans, and does not see how any combinations of his could be expected to result successfully except through implicit obedience.

These, and kindred expressions are interpolated in General Pope's communication. I shall not assume that propositions of the nature of truisms of no pertinency to the occasion, evidently pressed into service for a palpable purpose, need reference at your hands, or that of military men.

I do propose, if permitted to do so, to demonstrate by competent military authority, that in their opinion, but for the action and disposition of my corps during this eventful day of General Pope's campaign, not only would my own corps have been needlessly sacrificed, but his entire army put in such a plight as to be of no avail in the defence of the Capitol itself, which must then have been, in a great degree, left unguarded.

Although such demonstration is not necessary to my vindication as against General Pope's charges, it may awaken suggestions, the advantage of which I may at least partially claim.

In general terms throughout his letter, General Pope ignores the testimony given in my behalf of such officers as Generals Sykes, Heintzleman, Butterfield, J. F. Reynolds, Morell, Griffin, Ruggles, Locke, Weld, and others, whose career before and since my trial would warrant—I presume it is not too much to say—as much of credence as either the testimony or the opinion of General Pope is entitled to.

The witnesses on either side, having been more or less in the public service, have each a record that time or circumstances have established. I propose to add to the the list of those heretofore adduced by me, others of like prominence, equal integrity, bravery, and unimpeachability.

Should the commission I ask for be granted, General Pope will have an opportunity to add whatever of testimony he desires, both as to kind and amount.

I am aware of the tax a communication so lengthened—necessarily so—imposes upon you.

May I urge upon you to give me the opportunity I ask of vindication at the hands of the Government to which I have given my best years and of doing so promptly while actors and witnesses are yet in life.

I am sir,

With high respect,

Your obedient servant,

FITZ JOHN PORTER.

The following documents, in addition to some of the preceding are in possession of the Department.

NEW YORK, *January* 14, 1867.

To His Excellency, ANDREW JOHNSON, *President of the United States.*

SIR:—I beg leave to respectfully represent, that by Court Martial convened in Washington City in 1862, I was sentenced "to be cashiered, and forever rendered incapable of holding office under the Government of the United States," and that, in addition to all the penalties attached to so severe a sentence, persistent efforts have been made to fix those arising from the uncharged crime of treason.

Seventeen years of my life have been spent in the army of the United States—years covering the active events of the Mexican war, and including the opening and most trying years of the Rebellion. Intrusted at all times with duties of the greatest responsibilities, frequently performed at the peril of life, I can assert, without fear of denial, that up to the period of the presentation of the charges, no breath of suspicion had attached itself to a reputation which it had been, and still is, my life's study to preserve unsullied. I feel assured your Excellency will appreciate the motive that induces me to frankly say that, at no time from the presentation of the charges to the completion of the trial, did it occur to me that such a record as my country had generously permitted me to make, could I by any court be judged guilty of willfully neglecting the interests of that country in its hour of peril, and to whose reputation, history, and welfare I was bound by every sentiment of patriotism, gratitude, and interest.

Conscious of innocence, feeling that, whatever differences of opinion might arise upon other points, there would not and could not be any as to my faithfulness of purpose, I could not bring my mind to contemplate any other verdict than that of a speedy and honorable acquital.

It is possible I may have committed an error, both as to the Court and myself in thus assuming much that should have been set forth. I also feel assured that your Excellency will appreciate the motive that induces me to make reference to the events of my life while in my country's service. The vindication of my honor alone compels me to do so in this paper, as in a previous one read to the Court.

The verdict against me was found January, 1863, at a time of most unusual excitement. The country was environed with perils; distrust had seized upon many minds; errors of great magnitude had occurred; the press and forum vied with each other in responding to a great and growing sentiment that an example should be had by which faithlessness or incompetency should be promptly dealt with. May I not now say with truth that it was my misfortune to be charged and tried at this—to me—most inopportune of periods ?

I believe it is safe to say that much of the evidence adduced against me upon the trial would, in the light of the present full information upon the vital, and at the time necessarily disputed points, be either entirely changed or materially modified. Evidence of the most important character to me, at that time totally inaccessible to either the Court or myself, is now to be readily obtained, and in a form and under circumstances brought together that admit of no dispute. Competent and disinterested persons, including many of those who deemed my trial and condemnation just, now concur in the completeness of the vindication which this " unconscious testimony " has given me.

Relying on the justice of my government, feeling assured that with the return of peace calm feelings would prevail, and knowing that from the very nature of the case and the surroundings, time would, however slowly to my impatient honor, prove the best arbiter, I have borne in silence and without complaint the burden of that sentence.

I have taken the liberty of enclosing herewith certain documents from able and intelligent writers, which bear upon my case.*

* SWINTON's *Army of the Potomac,* GREELEY's *American Conflict,* an article by Mr. A. H. GUERNSEY, Editor *Pictorial History of the Rebellion.*

8

It is useless to say more than that they bear unsolicited confirmation so far as they go; and I believe the time is at hand when it is my duty to appeal to my government for a revision of my case, however nearly such a revision comes home to me and all I hold most sacred in my life.

It is a duty that I owe also to the honored officers who bore testimony in my behalf, to my brave command, whose history has been imperishably written, and to my country, that no stain of injustice shall be recorded against her.

My appeal is to your Excellency to appoint a court for the purpose of reconsidering the proceedings in my case, composed, as I trust it may be, of the best talent and most approved patriotism in the army.

I have every reason to believe that, with such a court now instituted, and with the full testimony now to be obtained, I can obtain the full and honorable acquittal I know I deserve; and which I shall ever seek at the hands of my country.

With high respect, I am your obedient servant,

FITZ JOHN PORTER.

The subjoined letters are filed with this appeal:

NATICK, Nov. 26, 1866.

To President Johnson :

SIR,—I have been informed that new evidence has been discovered touching the case of Fitz John Porter, late a Major-General in the volunteer forces of the United States. I cheerfully join with others in recommending the appointment of a commission, to consist of officers of acknowledged capacity and character, to examine the evidence and ascertain whether injustice has been done this officer or not, who, up to the time of the alleged offence, maintained the character of an officer of courage and ability.

Your obedient servant,

(Signed)   HENRY WILSON.

I think, with General Wilson, that a careful review, by a competent military commission, of the proceedings of the case of General Porter is an act of justice, and which, in trials before civil courts, is always granted as a matter of right. I trust his request will be granted.

(Signed)   JOHN SHERMAN.

I cheerfully unite with General Wilson in the within recommendation.

(Signed)   IRA HARRIS.

Senate Chamber, Jan. 16, 1867.

I concur.

(Signed)   HORACE GREELEY.

I cheerfully concur in the opinions above expressed.

(Signed)   L. F. S. FOSTER.

Jan. 17, 1867.

I concur, most cordially, in the recommendations of Senators Wilson, Sherman, Harris, and Foster, and express unreservedly my belief that a re-examination of this case is due to General Porter and the Government.

(Signed)   N. P. BANKS.

House of Representatives, Jan. 17, 1867.

Major-General Fitz John Porter was the first military officer sent by the Government to Harrisburg, at the beginning of the rebellion, and of the many who succeeded him, none of them were more zealous, faithful, and useful. I gave him my full confidence, and, from the high opinion I then formed of him, was surprised when his loyalty was doubted. Believing that subsequent events and evidence, not produced at his trial, fully justify a new trial, I very cordially and earnestly unite with Senator Wilson and other distinguished gentlemen, who concur with him in the within paper, in asking for General Porter the appointment of a new commission to hear his case, that justice may be done.

A. G. CURTIN.

Jan. 17, 1867.

To the President of the United States.

" Your memorialists respectfully represent that by a court-martial convened at Washington, Major-General Fitz John Porter was sentenced to be cashiered, 'and rendered forever incapable of service under the government of the United States.'

That such a sentence is to a gallant officer, in some respects worse than a sentence of death, inasmuch as it makes him the living and conspicuous victim of a terrible penalty.

That a few weeks before the terrible events which drew upon General Porter this severe sentence, he received the highest reward which the President can bestow, for skill and gallantry in one of the most important actions of the war.

Your memorialists are advised, that following the impulses of a controlling love of justice, your Excellency has, on many occasions during the war, reconsidered and revoked the sentences of court-martials in cases far less grave than the present, patiently employing your time, notwithstanding the urgent demands upon it, in sifting and weighing the evidence and listening to the explanations and defence of the accused.

And your memorialists in consideration of the extreme severity of the sentence in the case of Major-General Fitz John Porter, and of his previous high reputation, honorably earned on fields of peril and death, respectfully solicit you to reconsider the proceedings of the court-martial by which he was condemned.

This course, they beg leave to suggest, must, in whatever event, be satisfactory to your Excellency. Should the result be adverse to General Porter, it will strengthen you in the conviction that the original sentence was just. If favorable to the General, it will, your memorialists are confident, afford your generous nature the highest gratification which it is capable of enjoying.

EDWARD EVERETT,
ROBERT C. WINTHROP,
AMOS A. LAWRENCE,
GARDNER HOWLAND SHAW."

BOSTON, August, 1863.

BOSTON, *September* 21, 1867.

GENERAL:—At a meeting of the officers of the first division, 5th corps, called together to give an expression of sympathy at the death of our loved commander, General Griffin, the enclosed petition was presented and signed by all the officers present.

The duty of forwarding the document to you was entrusted to me, and in so doing I would say that I express the sentiments of most of those who served under General Porter in saying that they most earnestly desire that his request for a new trial be granted.

It was my fortune to be in command of a regiment in General Porter's corps, during that unfortunate campaign which ended in the battle of Bull Run, and having personal knowledge of many of the circumstances connected with his career, I have always felt that he was most unjustly dealt with.

Very respectfully yours,

L. STEPHENSON, JR.,
Late of 32nd Massachusetts Volunteers.

BOSTON, *September* 17, 1867.

The undersigned, who have served as officers of the fifth corps under General Fitz John Porter, respectfully, but urgently, request that the proceedings in his case may be revised, in accordance with the application which, they learn from the public press, he has addressed to the department.

Wm. S. Tilton, lately brevet brigadier general, United States volunteers.

A. P. Martin, late brevet colonel United States volunteers.

George M. Barnard, Jr., late brevet colonel eighteenth Massachusetts volunteers.

John W. Mahan, late major, ninth Massachusetts volunteers.

Aaron F. Walcott, late first lieutenant battery C, Massachusetts volunteers.

Francis J. Parker, colonel thirty-second Massachusetts infantry.

Geo. A. Batchelder, brevet lieutenant colonel twenty-second Massachusetts volunteers.

Mich. Scanlan, captain ninth Massachusetts volunteers.

P. T. Hanley, late lieutenant colonel ninth Massachusetts volunteers.

John M. Tobin, captain ninth Massachusetts volunteers.

James F. Moore, lieutenant second Maine volunteers.

Walter S. Davis, brevet lieutenant colonel twenty-second Massachusetts volunteers.

Louis N. Tucker, brevet major eighteenth Massachusetts volunteers.

Marcus M. Davis, captain twenty-second Massachusetts volunteers.

Thos. Sherwin, Jr., brevet brigadier general, late twenty-second Massachusetts volunteers.

L. Stephenson, Jr., brevet brigadier general, late thirty-second Massachusetts volunteers.

J. Cushing Edwards, brevet brigadier general, late thirty-second Massachusetts volunteers.

Chas. K. Cobb, first lieutenant and adjutant, late thirty-second Massachusetts volunteers.

Edward O. Shepard, brevet lieutenant colonel, late thirty-second Massachusetts volunteers.

Chris. Plunkett, late captain ninth Massachusetts volunteers.

Wm. M. Strachan, lieutenant and adjutant ninth Massachusetts volunteers.

Wm. M. Strachan, late captain ninth Massachusetts volunteers.

Chas. W. Thompson, first lieutenant thirty-ninth Massachusetts volunteers, formerly twelfth Massachusetts volunteers.

John F. Doherty, late captain ninth Massachusetts infantry.

P. E. Murphy, late first lieutenant ninth Massachusetts volunteers.

Wm. H. Gerty, late captain thirty-second Massachusetts volunteers.

B. F. Finan, late first lieutenant ninth Massachusetts infantry.

C. C. Bumpus, captain thirty-second Massachusetts volunteers, company B.

General U. S. Grant.

HARTFORD, CONNECTICUT, *September* 21, 1867.

My DEAR GRANT,—Fitz John Porter writes to me to ask that I will do something to aid him in getting a rehearing of his case. All that I can do is to write you, and give you the reasons why I think it will be an act of justice to give him the opportunity to clear himself from the terrible imputation now resting upon him.

I saw Porter in Pope's company the day after the latter's defeat at Bull Run, and afterwards, until we arrived in front of Washington. I know that they were on very cordial terms, and that Pope on some occasions advised with him confidentially. I talked a good deal myself with Pope, and I think that if he had had at that time any feeling that Porter had acted badly, I would have learned it then ; but I had no suspicion that he felt aggrieved at anything Porter or any one who was then near him had done. At Fairfax Court House, the day that we arrived at Washington, I noticed that Pope was particularly in good spirits and cordial with Porter. I have therefore always thought that the attack upon Porter was the result of an afterthought, and that the charges were not original with Pope.

During the trial, I thought it proper to inform Porter that Generals J. F. Reynolds, George H. Thomas, and myself would, if requested, go before the court and swear that we would not believe Pope or Roberts under oath. I had consulted General Reynolds before I made the proposition. He consented to go himself, and thought General Thomas would have no hesitation in giving such evidence. I was myself well convinced of General Thomas's opinion of Pope's veracity, from what I had often heard him say before the war. Porter declined to call us up to give this evidence, on the ground that the court appeared so well disposed towards him, and his case was going on so well, that he did not wish to irritate the court by an attempt to break down the evidence of the principal prosecutors. The sequel showed that he made a serious mistake.

But I think that the most equitable reason for a review of Porter's case is this : The Judge-Advocate-General, Holt, was the judge-advocate of the court. That was right enough. But no one will deny that a judge-advocate of a military court, when a prisoner is defended by able counsel, becomes to a great extent a prosecutor, and as such necessarily is biased against the prisoner. To say that General Holt was prejudiced against Porter is merely to say that he is like other men, and that he was so prejudiced the whole proceeding shows. Whether it is better or worse for the course of justice that the judge-advocate should be prejudiced has nothing to do with the question.

But an abstract of the proceedings and finding and sentence of the court had to be made by the Judge-Advocate-General for presentation to the President of the United States, upon which (for he necessarily could not read the evidence) he was to make up his mind as to the guilt or innocence of the accused. Was it right, proper, or decent that this abstract should be made up by the very man who had done his best to convict the prisoner? Did not such a proceeding prevent the President from learning any extenuating circumstance, or finding out anything weak in the evidence, if any such there were? Did it not, in fact, take away any chance from Porter which he might have had, had a cool, unbiased person of legal knowledge made this abstract, instead of General Holt.

The whole business seems to me like a prosecuting attorney passing sentence upon a prisoner in a civil court, immediately after the speeches of counsel. I think the fact that Mr. Lincoln had only general Holt's abstract to guide him, in making up an opinion on the proceedings of that court, is enough to invalidate the whole thing.

It has been said, and perhaps with truth, that there is no precedent to guide in this matter. It may be said with equal truth that never, since the trial of Admiral Byng, was injustice so without precedent done. I think that there never was a more appropriate opportunity for going beyond precedent, and establishing the fact that, no matter how or by whom flagrant injustice is done, you, when the power is in your hands, will see the right done.

For my part, I know that Porter was as loyal as the most loyal soldier now dead, and that no thought of treason or disaffection entered his brain. He was a victim to Pope's failure in Virginia, and it seems to me he has remained a victim long enough. You will, in my opinion, do an act which will not be the least among those which will make up your fame, if you will lend your weight towards giving Porter the opportunity to retrieve his character as a citizen and soldier.

I am truly your friend,

W. B. FRANKLIN.

General U. S. GRANT,
Commanding Army of the United States.